THE POWER OF ETHNIC MEDIA

A HOW-TO GUIDE FOR
COMMUNICATION PROFESSIONALS

Yurina Melara

Copyright © 2023 Yurina Melara
All rights reserved.
ISBN: 9798861832960

No part of this book may be reproduced, or stored in a retrieval system, or transmitted in any form or by any means, electronic, mechanical, photocopying, recording, or otherwise, without express written permission of the publisher.

Cover design by: Art Painter
Printed in the United States of America

DEDICATION

To my colleagues in the newsrooms.

To my colleagues in PR agencies.

To my colleagues on the streets and on their phones.

To my colleagues who do the right thing day in, day out.

TABLE OF CONTENTS

	Acknowledgments	i
1	One Size Does Not Fit All	3
2	Defining Ethnic Media	13
3	A Brief History of Ethnic Media in the US	22
4	The Why is Always a Must	34
5	How to Target Audiences through Ethnic Media	42
6	How to Establish Credibility Using Ethnic Media	52
7	Media Relations: Building Relations	61
8	Challenges When Working with Ethnic Media Outlets	65
9	A Case Study	79
	About the Author	101

ACKNOWLEDGMENTS

This guide is possible thanks to the patient guidance of my Beta Readers.

Thank you!

CHAPTER 1

One Size Does Not Fit All

"Can you tell me what you do? Do you translate?" The high-ranking communications official asked me, following my introduction as a multiethnic public relations professional. Even after 20+ years on the job, I still froze. Here was yet another organization that treated ethnic media as an afterthought, rather than an incredibly valuable tool to build trust with their audiences. I knew at that moment that I wouldn't get the job.

Many institutions have been advised to diversify their teams and audiences, with external vendors often being consulted to fulfill this goal. Regrettably, despite the evidence presented, some officials balk at the price tag of bringing on extra staff and this opportunity to strengthen their communications portfolio is lost.

Like the previous scenario, a senior official failed to understand the positive impact of having a multiethnic approach to their campaigns. I did my best to explain, but after just a couple of minutes, she thanked me and got off the phone.

I'm writing this manual to help those senior officials broaden their views, and also for those communication professionals who would like to know how we all can contribute to our line of work.

Overall, the objective of this manual is to highlight the importance of incorporating ethnic media outlets into the framework of public relations and public educational campaigns, particularly in states characterized by substantial immigrant populations, such as California, New York, Arizona, Texas, New

Orleans, Washington DC suburbs, and Florida. In these regions, the presence of numerous immigrants calls for a comprehensive understanding of the role ethnic media plays in effective communication strategies.

Nationally, the Census Bureau estimates that around 13.6 percent of the population is foreign-born. Remarkably, in California, one out of every four residents are an immigrant, and in Florida, this ratio stands at about one in every five individuals. Moreover, the Census reveals that a significant 10% of the total population, roughly 33 million people, self-identify as "multiracial and/or multiethnic." Nationally, about 1 in 5 people speak other language than English at home. In, my state of California, is about 40% of the population.

To put it in context, the United States is home to more immigrants, approximately 45 million, than the entire population of Canada, which hovers around 38 to 39 million people. This emphasizes the pivotal role of understanding and harnessing the potential of these diverse communities for effective communication and engagement strategies.

The last pandemic showed us how much we all needed ethnic media to get to the hard to reach in-language communities. Latinos were almost half of all COVID cases and African American and Latinos were dying at a higher rate than any other segments.

Let's go back to 2020-2021, the rapidly changing COVID-19 guidelines, evolving research, and the urgent need for behavioral change required for an information dissemination system that could keep pace. It quickly became evident that not all communities were receiving the same level of attention from mainstream media. Language barriers, cultural differences, and historical mistrust of the healthcare system created gaps in the communication chain, leaving some communities more vulnerable to the COVID-19 virus.

Recognizing this challenge, some communication professionals in state agencies began to explore ethnic media outlets to bridge these gaps. Ethnic media, including newspapers, radio stations, television channels, and online platforms, serve specific communities with news and information in their native languages. This unique position made them ideal partners in the fight against COVID-19.

My background

In March 2000, I arrived from El Salvador to Los Angeles, California, with two bags, a dog, a recent but almost failing marriage, and $1,000 that I borrowed from my mother. Less than a month later, I was hired as the assistant to the editor for the Spanish section of the *Wave Community Newspapers*, called *La Ola*, which was in the heart of south-central Los Angeles. My previous job was as a reporter for a daily newspaper in San Salvador, El Salvador, and going from a daily to weekly was a mental relief, although it took me a moment to get used to my new adopted city, and the geographical distances. Overall, I was lucky to find a job so quickly in such a big and diverse metropolis.

By May of that same year, the editor I was working for had left the weekly newspaper, and I thought I was going to lose my new job. So, I did what I always do: I kept going.

With my resume in one hand and my most convincing voice, I knocked on the door of the Executive Editor of the *Wave*. I asked him to let me take over the two-page edition of *La Ola*, while he searched for a new editor. I told him that for the last two weeks, before my editor left, I was also writing stories and helping copy edit the edition. He decided to try. Thinking back, I believe he did not have much of an option due to how fast the Spanish editor left. I was there, and I was already doing most of the job.

A month later, once it was obvious, I was doing all the work, and he offered me the position. During the five years I was the Spanish editor, I took *La Ola* from a couple of pages inside the *Wave* to a standalone weekly tabloid with its own sports column, community highlights and a strong local Hispanic entertainment coverage. And, of course, its own distribution route in South Los Angeles and other surrounding areas that were becoming increasingly Spanish-speaking new-immigrant neighborhoods.

I was so happy. It was my first baby. Plus, I had my real first baby in 2003 while I was working on the dissertation for my Ph.D. in Philosophy of Natural Health.

It was hard for me to leave La Ola, but in May 2005, I received an offer at *La Opinión*, the largest daily Spanish newspaper in the country. At the same time —that same month— I finished all the requisites for the Ph.D.

While at *La Opinión*, and for a brief period, I also helped produce a couple of television shows in a smaller Spanish television station. Later, in 2009 and for about six months, I also produced and anchored my own television show. It was fun. Everything related to the media is fun for me.

But throughout all those 15 years in Spanish media, I didn't realize that I was working in "ETHNIC MEDIA."

Yes, very naïve of me, but it was all I knew. Of course, I knew there was English media, Chinese media, Vietnamese media, and other ethnicities, but to me, it was only "MEDIA."

It was only then that I learned that for public relations (PR) professionals, adverting, government, and mainstream media, any content in other language or for a specific group is labeled as "ethnic," which has an stigma attached, and a connotation of "lesser value." I learned about this distinction in 2016, when I went to work for a state agency as a Public Information Officer.

Since then, I have specialized in what communications experts' call *Ethnic Media*.

But I really must emphasize that for those in newsrooms that produce news stories in other languages, they don't see themselves as ethnic media. Those who do this work daily see themselves as journalists and media outlets committed to informing and educating communities about how to navigate life in the United States, to better our lives and achieve the American Dream. Whatever version of the American Dream we have.

That's the reason our stories are different, our angles are different, and our mission is different.
It's important that communication professionals understand and learn how to engage with diverse audiences and meet their needs for information.

This book summarizes the history and development of ethnic media, examines the various types of media available, and offers practical advice on using ethnic media effectively to reach and engage diverse audiences.

It also looks at the challenges and opportunities of working with ethnic media and offers strategies for building relationships with media outlets and audiences.

This book is a resource for anyone looking to better understand and engage with immigrants, refugees, and diverse audiences leveraging ethnic media.

CHAPTER 2

Defining Ethnic Media

"Why are we spending so much time in a tiny publication?" a campaign strategist asked in an annoyed tone. She went on explaining that in the past, she worked at publications that were larger, and she didn't understand why we were spending so much time figuring out what we were doing, and why it had to be in English and Spanish. *"Let's just do Spanish and get it over with,"* she recommended.

In terms of copies sold and distributed, it might have seemed to be as a tiny publication for her, but it was the newspaper of record for that community. Clearly, this was just another case of myopia toward ethnic media.

The Power of Ethnic Media

Ethnic media encompasses media platforms tailored to distinct ethnic or cultural communities. Although these outlets might appear relatively modest when contrasted with mainstream market channels, they play a pivotal role by offering news, information, and entertainment in their native languages.

When examining language preferences among immigrants, a noteworthy pattern emerges approximately one-third of immigrants predominantly communicate in their native language, another third is bilingual, while the remaining third is exclusively monolingual[1].

Ethnic media can include newspapers, magazines, radio stations, television channels, websites, and social media platforms. Most have a combination of all the above platforms.

---

[1] "Languages spoken among U.S. immigrants, 2018." Pew Research Center. https://www.pewresearch.org/hispanic/chart/languages-spoken-among-u-s-immigrants-2018/

The Power of Ethnic Media

These outlets are often used to provide news that people can use, like immigration information and tips. It can also include entertainment and culture. Some media outlets are firm believers of furthering the education of their community members and hold literacy workshops or even book competitions.

In general, ethnic media in the United States serve diverse communities such as Hispanic/Latino, African American, Asian American, Native American, and other communities.

It is common for ethnic media outlets to provide a platform for members of that community to express their opinions and perspectives. This can be especially important for people who are trying to understand or navigate the new way to do things.

In-language media outlets also provide a way for members of their communities to stay connected to their culture.

The Power of Ethnic Media

Often, English-only Americans struggle to understand any or all aspects of ethnic media outlets, like the example above, simply because they are not exposed to them regularly, and this is not how mainstream outlets function.

The outlets can also provide a platform for people to learn more about their history and culture, and how to stay in touch with other people with similar experiences. Ethnic media plays a significant role in serving the informational needs of ethnic communities.

They help to bridge language and cultural barriers, provide a sense of community, and foster cultural preservation and identity. They also serve as a platform for community engagement, advocacy, and empowerment.

The management of ethnic media varies depending on the outlet and community it serves. However, some common features of ethnic media include:

Language and cultural relevance: Ethnic media operates primarily in languages distinct from English and concentrates on subjects that hold significance within the particular ethnic community it caters to. This form of media delivers news, information, and entertainment meticulously customized to align with the cultural sensibilities and interests of its intended audience.

Consider the linguistic diversity within public schools, where students in cities like Los Angeles or New York converse in over 28 languages. This statistic underscores the composition of today's youth in the US and prompts contemplation of the potential market share. For instance, major corporations like Walmart[2] strategically engage in language-specific outlets, employing a multitude of channels to communicate with diverse audiences. Similarly,

---

[2] "An Update on Our DEI Efforts in Marketing." Walmart press release. May 2021. https://corporate.walmart.com/news/2021/05/21/an-update-on-our-dei-efforts-in-marketing

entities such as Ford[3], whether in relation to vehicles or insurance companies, recognize the value of such tailored communication. This accentuates the relevance for US marketers to harness the potency of ethnic media outlets, leading to a thought-provoking comparison: if capitalists recognize their value, shouldn't we all?

Community-oriented content: Ethnic media often covers local news and events, community stories, and cultural content that interests the target ethnic community. It may also provide coverage of news and events from the home country or region of the community.

Community engagement: Ethnic media serves as a platform for community engagement, providing a voice to the ethnic community and facilitating communication and interaction among community members. It often covers community events,

---

[3] "Core support for the Center for Community and Ethnic Media." Ford Foundation. April 2023. https://www.fordfound.org/work/our-grants/awarded-grants/awarded-grant/

promotes community initiatives, and encourages community participation.

Advocacy and empowerment: Ethnic media may engage in advocacy on behalf of the ethnic community it serves, raising awareness of community issues, advocating for policy changes, and promoting social and political empowerment. This is the perfect chance to create earned media content. Providing all the pieces for the journalist to assemble the story will make it easier for them to write it. Does your campaign have an empowerment or advocacy angle? Explore it.

Advertising and revenue generation: When you're putting your budget together, remember that ethnic media relies on advertising and other revenue sources to sustain its operations. It's a popular way for businesses trying to reach out to particular ethnic groups, as well as government departments, non-profits, and community associations, to advertise. In the process of crafting your media procurement strategy, it's prudent to inquire about the absence of language-specific ethnic outlets. Such an omission prompts the query: Why the oversight? Certain advertising firms may assert that purchasing "multicultural" slots encompasses a broad spectrum of segments. This assertion, however, does not hold true. Such an approach amounts to procuring general-market content veiled as something it is not.

Multi-platform presence: Ethnic media may have a presence across multiple media channels, including print, radio, television, websites, and social media platforms, to reach its target audience through various means of communication.

Cultural preservation and identity: Ethnic media frequently assumes a pivotal role in safeguarding and advancing the cultural distinctiveness of the specific ethnic enclave it caters to. This encompasses aspects such as language, time-honored practices, customs, and ancestral legacy. Additionally, the reinforcement of the "mother tongue" within these media outlets not only serves to uphold cultural heritage but also paves the way for an enriched linguistic and cultural panorama. By embracing and perpetuating diverse languages, the broader US populace becomes equipped to explore other cultures, thereby fostering an expanded US market. This broader cultural and linguistic acumen empowers "Americans" to forge global connections.

Remember, your campaign can benefit and reach a larger audience, given that you understand their purpose, and you are willing to open your mind to the possibility that there is a cultural component involved in a communications campaign.

Now that you know the important roles ethnic media serve in the community, let's look at the legacy of ethnic media in the U.S.

CHAPTER 3

A Brief History of Ethnic Media in the United States (U.S.)

The history of ethnic media in the United States is long and complex, with a variety of outlets, languages and formats emerging over the years to serve the needs of different communities.

From the earliest days of the nation, ethnic media has been an important part of the American experience, providing a platform for minority voices to be heard and for diverse perspectives to be shared. In the early 19th century, the first wave of ethnic media emerged as newspapers and magazines. These publications served as a way for immigrants to stay connected to their home countries and to share news and information with one another.[4]

The first ethnic newspaper in the United States was the German-language *Der Weltburger*, which was founded in 1836.[5] This publication was followed by several other publications such as the Chinese-language *Chung Sai Yat Po* in 1900[6], and the Spanish-language *La Prensa* in 1913, which is now part of *Impremedia*, an independent news conglomerate that owns *La Opinión*, historically one of the most influential newsrooms in the country[7].

The second wave of ethnic media began in the early 20th century with the rise of radio and television. These new technologies allowed for the dissemination

---

[4] Thompson, John B. (1995). The Media and Modernity: A Social Theory of the Media. Stanford University Press.

[5] Weinryb Groshsaal, Lean. "German Newspapers and the Growth of the American Ethnic Press. 7/2/2014. https://www.neh.gov/divisions/preservation/featured-project/chronicling-americas-historic-german-newspapers-and-the-grow

[6] Chiu, Kuei. "Asian Language Newspapers in the United States: History Revisited." Asian Studies, Humanities and Arts Bibliographer University of California, Riverside. 11/12/2008

[7] "El Diario La Prensa." Wikipedia. https://en.wikipedia.org/wiki/El_Diario_La_Prensa

of news and information to a much wider audience, and ethnic media outlets quickly adopted them.

In the 1940s radio stations like KWKW in Los Angeles[8] initiated Spanish-language broadcasts, marking a significant cultural shift, and *Univision*'s first Texan station can be traced back to 1946[9]. Similarly, the establishment of the first Chinese-language television station, KTSF, in San Francisco, took place in 1976[10], further contributing to the diversification of media.

Notably, Univision's viewership surpasses that of numerous US-based stations, underscoring its substantial audience reach[11]. A comparative analysis

---

[8] "KWKW." Wikipedia. https://en.wikipedia.org/wiki/KWKW

[9] "THE HISTORY OF SERVING HISPANIC AMERICA." TelevisaUnivision website. https://corporate.televisaunivision.com/timeline/

[10] "KTSF Celebrates 30 Years as the Nation's Leading Asian Broadcaster". Archived from the original on February 18, 2010. Retrieved February 13, 2011.

[11] Romero, Mark Hugo, & Ramírez, A. Chris. (2008). The Growing Hispanic Population in the United States. Pew Hispanic Center Report.

of viewership against major networks like CBS and PBS reveals this trend[12].

The third phase of ethnic media emerged in the latter part of the 20th century, coinciding with the advent of the internet. This epoch saw the birth of diverse online platforms, including websites, blogs, and social media channels, reshaping the media landscape.

It's worth exploring the extent of native language usage on popular platforms like Facebook and Twitter, shedding light on the linguistic diversity within digital spaces.

This phenomenon has amplified access to international media outlets, facilitating cross-cultural interactions. Along the US-Mexico border, bilingual messaging extends across border regions, effectively bridging both sides of the divide. The strategic dissemination of information in this manner warrants

---

[12] Romero, Mark Hugo, & Ramírez, A. Chris. (2008). The Growing Hispanic Population in the United States. Pew Hispanic Center Report.

further exploration, reflecting the nuanced dynamics of ethnic media's evolving impact.

These outlets have allowed for the sharing of news and information unprecedentedly, and have been especially important for minority communities, who often lack access to traditional media outlets and could feel isolated because of language barriers.

As of this first publication, in 2023, ethnic media continues to play an important role in the United States. As our country grows ever more diverse, our communications require a diversity of content. Mainstream media still has much to learn about how to ensure all voices are heard and diverse perspectives shared. Ethnic media will continue to bridge the gap between mainstream media and the needs of the rest of our communities, particularly the monolingual and/or marginalized.

As the nation continues to become more diverse, by 2050. Latinos will be the largest minority; ethnic media will continue to be an important part of the American experience[13].

The last pandemic of COVID-19 proved the value of ethnic media, as most outlets came out against the misinformation that was spreading like wildfire, and which threatened the lives of low-income immigrant non-English-speaking communities even more. On Chapter 9, we will dive in.

The evolution of ethnic media platforms:

Civil Rights Era and Social Movements: In the 20th century, ethnic media played a vital role during the Civil Rights Movement and other social movements. Many books have been written on the pivotal role that black newspapers had during the Civil Rights era. The same is true for Spanish publications covering discrimination stories or labor union struggles. I will not attempt to summarize those

---

[13] Passel, Jeffrey S., and Cohn, D'vera. "U.S. Population Projections: 2005-2050." 2/11/2008. https://www.pewresearch.org/hispanic/2008/02/11/us-population-projections-2005-2050/

academic books/publications already in existence. Just a quick reminder that this is not a historical research project. **This is an easy-to-use guide.**

Mainstream Media Diversification: In recent decades, there has been a growing recognition of the need for diversity and representation in the mainstream media. As a result, several mainstream media outlets have established dedicated sections or programs targeting ethnic communities. These efforts have aimed to provide coverage of issues relevant to ethnic communities, increase representation in the media, and cater to the diverse information needs of these communities. An example of how it has entered mainstream is the "Emerging Communities" beat in KPCC, part of the NPR radio network.

Digital Media and Social Media: digital media and social media have significantly affected the landscape of ethnic media in the United States. Many ethnic media outlets have moved online or established a strong presence on social media platforms to reach wider audiences and engage with their communities.

Digital and social media have provided new opportunities for ethnic media to disseminate news and information, connect with communities, and amplify voices. Also we also must acknowledge that podcasts have also emerged as a dynamic medium within ethnic media. Notably, PBS has been home to "*Latino USA*" for over three and a half decades, representing a remarkable instance of ethnic media in English. This facet deserves acknowledgment alongside the bilingual and Spanglish initiatives that have been undertaken. Efforts to incorporate these linguistic variations highlight a concerted endeavor to authentically represent and engage with diverse audiences.

Commercialization and Professionalization: Ethnic media in the United States has also witnessed commercialization and professionalization over the years. Many ethnic media outlets have transitioned from community-based grassroots efforts to professional news organizations with paid staff, advertising revenues, and a wider reach. This has allowed for increased sustainability and growth, however, since these are smaller institutions the paid/earned division that exists in mainstream media is very slim, and often the line can be blurry.

If you think you can separate paid from earned efforts with these outlets, you are in for a surprise.

In ethnic publications like African American, Armenian, Caribbean, smaller Spanish publications and many Asian language outlets, there is no difference. The publisher typically plays the role of the reporter and advertising representative and will often ask for ad support for the publication. Let me be clear, you are not buying a story or buying coverage, you are making sure the publication/outlet stays open and hearing your message. Publishers will not write stories they do not believe will help their communities.

Also, in an era marked by the shifting tides of climate patterns and the increasing frequency of weather-related calamities, a new weather reality has dawned upon us. The urgency of emergency preparedness takes center stage, offering a crucial lifeline in the face of potential catastrophes. In this evolving landscape, the significance of multilingual communication cannot be overstated.

Consider the scenario: a looming hurricane, an imminent wildfire, or a sudden flood. The ability to disseminate timely and accurate information can mean the difference between life and death, security, and chaos.

However, the challenge arises when a diverse population, encompassing various ethnic backgrounds and languages, is at risk. If essential messages fail to reach individuals in their preferred languages, a hazardous gap emerges, hindering effective disaster response and recovery efforts.

This sobering truth underscores the vital role of ethnic media outlets in this context. These channels possess the unique capability to bridge linguistic divides, ensuring that critical information resonates with all members of society. The power of culturally tailored messages cannot be underestimated. By communicating in languages that communities understand and relate to, the resonance and impact of emergency directives are heightened, transcending linguistic barriers, and enabling swift and coordinated action.

The imperative for embracing multilingual emergency communication extends beyond altruism; it rests upon a foundation of self-interest. Government agencies tasked with safeguarding their citizenry are more equipped to fulfill their duty when their constituents are well-informed and empowered to respond effectively. Similarly, businesses vested in risk management and public safety, such as insurance carriers, recognize that proactive multilingual engagement enhances their ability to mitigate losses and protect their assets.

Ultimately, the new weather reality demands a holistic approach to emergency preparedness—one that recognizes the paramount importance of multilingual communication through ethnic media outlets. As we navigate a future fraught with climatic uncertainties, the cultivation of linguistic inclusivity emerges not only as a moral imperative but also as a strategic imperative, serving the interests of both governance and enterprise. In embracing this ethos, we fortify our collective resilience and strengthen our ability to weather the storms that lie ahead.

When we all live by this belief, we become stronger together and can handle anything that comes our way.

CHAPTER 4

The Why is Always a Must

"Why are you asking about our media buy? I'm talking about setting up a press conference with ethnic media outlets," one of the communication's supervisors asked me.

So, I had to stop and explain, again, that with ethnic media one must not separate the earned and paid components. When we are trying to reach out to these hard to reach in-language communities, we need to know where the budget is going and make sure to match it with the invites. If you have a budget to hire a PR company, you have an usable budget.

Keep this tip in mind when you are doing a regionalized targeted press event with small ethnic media outlets.

When you are doing a large statewide or nationwide event, this tip doesn't matter, and reporters from bigger outlets like *Univision, Telemundo, Skylink, Crossing TV* and *La Opinión*, won't wonder about the budget. In terms of separation between their sales and newsrooms departments, they operate similarly to mainstream media reporters.

The combination of public relations and advertising when connecting with ethnic media is an essential part of any strategic communication plan for organizations intending to interact with ethnic communities in the United States.

Just to quickly define concepts: Public Relations (PR) is the practice of managing communication between an organization and its target audiences to build relationships, enhance reputation, and convey messages effectively. PR is commonly known as earned media efforts. Meanwhile, paid media refers to advertising or promotional content that is paid for by an organization to reach a wider audience.

When working with media outlets, organizations often use both PR and paid media as separate tools, but when working with ethnic media, it is a MUST to combine both strategies to communicate the messages effectively and build relationships with the targeted ethnic communities.

Here are some key points to consider in the intersection of earned and paid when working with ethnic media:

Media outreach and relationship building: PR professionals can engage with ethnic media outlets through media outreach efforts, including pitching story ideas, providing press releases or media advisories, and arranging interviews or appearances. Building relationships with editors, reporters, and producers in ethnic media can help organizations establish a powerful presence and gain credibility within the targeted ethnic communities.

Content creation and localization: PR professionals can work with ethnic media to create content that is relevant and resonates with the cultural sensibilities of the target ethnic community. This may include translating press materials or developing content that reflects the cultural nuances and interests of the community. Paid media can also promote this localized content, such as sponsored articles or social media posts, to reach a wider audience within the ethnic community.

Recently, I saw a billboard of a community clinic in Koreatown, Los Angeles, that featured a white doctor with an old Asian lady. My first thought was, "How are they communicating?" The billboard had a headline in Korean, and the old lady was smiling. There is no doubt in my mind that the person who composed the art was not Korean, nor did they have access to a Korean PR/Advertising expert because if they did, they would have made sure the art represented their community.

Advertising and sponsored content: Paid media complement PR efforts by utilizing advertising or sponsored content in ethnic media outlets to increase visibility and reach among the target audience. This may include sponsored articles, or sponsored social media posts that are specifically designed to engage with the ethnic community and convey key messages or promote products/services.

Targeted audience segmentation: Earned and paid media can work together to segment the target audience within the ethnic community based on demographics, interests, or behaviors. This allows organizations to tailor their messages and paid media efforts to reach effectively and resonate with the specific segments of the ethnic community they are trying to engage with.

Monitoring and measurement: Earned and paid media efforts should be monitored and measured to evaluate their effectiveness in reaching the intended goals. PR professionals can use media monitoring tools to track coverage and sentiment in ethnic media outlets, while paid media efforts can be measured through metrics such as reach, engagement, and conversions.

Cultural sensitivity and genuine communication: In the realm of ethnic media engagement, fostering genuine and culturally sensitive communication is of paramount importance. Public relations experts must approach their interactions with a keen awareness of cultural subtleties, language preferences, and community norms. This approach ensures that the messages conveyed are not only respectful but also deeply resonate with the specific ethnic group being targeted.

Within this context, paid media efforts must be meticulously crafted with authenticity as a guiding principle, unlike the previous Korean clinic example. The aim is to sidestep cultural misappropriation or any inadvertent insensitivity, both of which have the potential to cast a detrimental shadow over an organization's reputation and its rapport with the community it seeks to engage.

It is here that the imperative to enlist individuals from within these communities becomes evident. This underscores the significance of hiring personnel, if possible, who intimately understand the dynamics and nuances of the targeted ethnic audience. Moreover, it emphasizes the intrinsic diversity within these communities, reminding us that messages need to mirror this diversity, both in content and in the individuals delivering them.

To illustrate, utilizing a Caribbean-accented Spanish speaking Cuban announcer to convey a message to Spanish-speaking Mexicans norteño farmworkers in a small town in Texas o California, or featuring a Vietnamese representative in a Chinese advertisement can ring as dissonant and inauthentic.

These instances underscore the importance of matching the right communicator to the right audience, thereby ensuring a harmonious alignment between the message, the messenger, and the recipient.

Basically, to really engage with ethnic media, you must try to understand and connect with all the different cultures that make up our social lives. We're not just being respectful of different cultures, we're also making sure our messages are diverse, accurate, and relatable. That way, we can build actual relationships while respecting our diverse society.

CHAPTER 5

How to Target Audiences through Ethnic Media

"Let's just sponsor the Mexican Parade. I think that would be enough for Hispanic Heritage Month, right?" someone said in a planning meeting after I proposed we do another community activations in September.

I explained that even though Mexicans are the largest Hispanic ethnic group in California, there is another large Hispanic community that also celebrates its independence in September, the Central Americans. Their Independence Day is on September 15th, while the Mexican Independence celebration is on September 16th.

Targeting audiences using ethnic media outlets requires a strategic approach that takes into consideration the unique characteristics and preferences of the ethnic communities being targeted, and sometimes even subgroups within the ethnic group, like the example in this chapter.

To continue with our how-to guide, here are some steps for targeting audiences effectively using ethnic media outlets:

Comprehend the Ethnic Community: Do your research to really understand the ethnic group you want to work with. This means making sure you understand their language, culture, values, traditions, and media habits. Immerse yourself in an exploration of the demographics, interests, and proclivities of the target audience encompassed within the ethnic community. Employ this knowledge to meticulously tailor your messages, recognizing the intricate demographic composition, language preferences, and diverse subgroups that characterize these communities. We need to embrace the beautiful intricacies within every ethnicity. For instance, it's important to acknowledged the multitude of subgroups within the Asian community—numbering more than 53— and recognizing the distinctiveness that sets apart Africans, African Americans, and the expansive diversity inherent in African cultures. The list goes on.

In California, not all Spanish speakers are Mexicans. In New York City not everyone is from Puerto Rico, neither are all Hispanics Cubans or Colombians in Florida. This knowledge and understanding could be the foundation for a successful campaign that resonates with people.

It is crucial to note that if you cannot fully immerse yourself, it may be beneficial to collaborate with agencies that specialize in and comprehend the distinctive differences and attributes of diverse communities, especially when communicating with AAPI and Native American audiences. In the US, 23.5 million people are being classified as AAPI, a term that comprises many distinct languages, cultures, and customs[14]. And for Native American audiences, please make sure that you work with someone who comes from those communities and understands all the nuances. It is complicated, and there are different levels of sensitives that no one should ignore.

Identify Relevant Ethnic Media Outlets: Identify ethnic media outlets that are popular and trusted within the target community. As discussed previously, don't limit yourself to one platform and be sure to consider newspapers, magazines, radio stations, TV stations, websites, social media pages, and other digital platforms that cater to the ethnic community you are targeting. Research their reach, readership, viewership, and engagement levels to ensure they align with your target audience.

To illustrate, if you look to conduct a campaign geared towards pregnant women in South Los

---

[14] "AAPI Demographics: Data on Asian American Ethnicities, Geography, Income and Education." US Facts. https://usafacts.org/articles/the-diverse-demographics-of-asian-americans/

Angeles because of an elevated fatality rate, realize that many of the Latinos in that region come from El Salvador, Guatemala and Honduras, and that instead of tuning into the main Spanish language newscast, they might get their news from the Central American TV programs that, in most cases, are produced locally for them by them.

Cultivate Cultural Proficiency: Foster a deep sense of cultural proficiency when engaging with ethnic media platforms. To achieve success, one must possess a thorough knowledge of the cultural nuances, sensitivities, and communication norms of the target community. Employ language, tone, and visuals that seamlessly align with the cultural backdrop of the community, resonating in an authentic manner. It's important to be cautious and respectful when crafting messages, avoiding assumptions or stereotypes.

If within your means, consider investing in focus group research to refine your approach. However, it's paramount that such research accurately mirrors the genuine audience you intend to connect with.

Once, I participated in a focus group supposedly tailored for Spanish speakers in California, yet over half of the attendees were not proficient native Spanish speakers, despite their Spanish surnames, leading the research agency to inaccurately portray them as Spanish-dominant Latinos. This scenario underscores the necessity of ensuring that research efforts authentically mirror the target audience, encapsulating their true linguistic and cultural nuances.

Basically, being culturally proficient means paying attention to the little things and really trying to understand and appreciate the diverse mix of different ethnic groups.

The messaging should be genuine and respectful to build a strong relationship with these communities.

Customize Your Message: Tailor your messages to resonate with the target community. Consider the language, cultural references, and values that are relevant to the community. Highlight how your product, service, or message is specifically relevant to the needs, interests, and aspirations of the community. Use testimonials, success stories, and real-life examples that are relatable to the community.

Build Relationships with Ethnic Media Outlets: Establish relationships with ethnic media outlets to build trust and credibility. Engage with them through regular communication, provide them with relevant and timely news or story ideas, and offer to be a resource for their coverage. Collaborate on content creation, interviews, or guest appearances to increase your visibility within the ethnic community.

Leverage Advertising Opportunities: Placing paid content in ethnic newspapers, magazines, radio stations, TV stations, websites, or social media pages will increase your visibility and reach within the target community. Work with the media outlet to customize your advertisements to fit their audience and messaging style. In most cases, the outlets are happy to help and would do it for free.

Participate in Community Initiatives and Collaborations: Whenever possible embrace community initiatives and collaborative ventures to forge robust relationships and bolster your standing within the ethnic community. Immerse yourself in cultural festivals, communal assemblies, and pertinent occasions of significance to the target community. Forge partnerships with local entities, influencers, or community figures to magnify the reach of your message and foster a foundation of trust. A case in point from the past exemplifies the significance of such collaborations.

And to editorialized on past successful PR campaigns, let's look at the tobacco industry, who did an exceptional outreach extending their financial support to various community groups. This financial tie often led to a compromised ability for these groups to voice concerns about the detrimental impact of tobacco within the community. This illustrates how industries can garner support through financial contributions, potentially leading to a hesitance to address certain adverse consequences.

Similarly, public health and education institutions can follow those outreach practices to advance their public-interest missions. By proactively sponsoring community events, educational initiatives, and health campaigns, they can solidify a positive presence and secure a platform from which to effectively communicate their vital messages.

Be aware that community engagement and partnerships serve as a pivotal means to foster rapport, credibility, and resonance within ethnic communities.

Monitor and Evaluate Results: Regularly monitor and evaluate the effectiveness of your efforts in targeting audiences using ethnic media outlets. Track metrics such as reach, engagement, feedback, and conversions, to assess the impact of your messages. Adjust your approach based on feedback and insights gained from your evaluation to optimize your targeting efforts.

By following these steps and taking a strategic approach, you can effectively target audiences using ethnic media outlets and establish meaningful connections with the ethnic communities you are trying to reach.

Remember that it's important to be culturally sensitive, respectful, and genuine in your approach to build trust and credibility within the community.

CHAPTER 6

How To Establish Credibility Using Ethnic Media

Establishing credibility using ethnic media outlets requires a strategic approach that considers the unique characteristics and dynamics of those outlets.

Here are some steps to consider:

1. **Understand the target audience:** Each ethnic media outlet serves a specific community with its own cultural, linguistic, and social nuances. Understanding the target audience of the ethnic media outlet you want to establish credibility with is critical. Research their interests, needs, values, and concerns, and tailor your message accordingly to resonate with their experiences and perspectives.
   For example: If you are targeting Latinos, you need to understand that we value family, but

family is not limited to mom, dad and kids. Family includes uncles, grandma or second cousins and his/her children, who are considered nieces and nephews. Their life experience and expectations are different if they are from new immigrants, second or third generation, and the country of origin is also crucial when doing a targeted campaign. This must be taken into consideration.

2. **Build relationships:** Building relationships with the editorial staff and journalists of the ethnic media outlet is key to establishing credibility. Attend events, seminars, and conferences organized by the outlet, and engage in conversations with the journalists. Offer yourself as a resource on topics relevant to their audience and provide valuable insights and perspectives. Be respectful, authentic, and patient in building these relationships over time.
Quick story: In 2015, *La Opinión* endorsed then California Attorney General, Kamala Harris for the U.S. Senate over Latina Democratic rival Representative Loretta

Sánchez, of Garden Grove[15]. Why? Simple… Harris took the time to attend the Spanish newspaper's cocktail celebration of their new marketing campaign. She was charming and made her case in person to the editorial board during a very relaxed event. Her competition did not show up. I was there to witness history in the making.

3. **Provide accurate and relevant content:** Crafting content for ethnic media outlets requires a keen focus on accuracy, relevance, and resonance with their audience. Ensure that your content is thoroughly researched, meticulously fact-checked, and harmoniously aligned with the values and interests of the community being served by the media outlet. Refrain from employing generic or stereotypical messaging, opting instead to tailor your materials to the precise cultural and linguistic nuances of the ethnic media platform. In addition to this, consider proactively assisting the outlets by providing them with *ready-to-use content* that they can

---

[15] Kamala Harris lands La Opinión endorsement for Senate. Los Angeles Times. Oct. 2015. https://www.latimes.com/local/political/la-me-pc-kamala-harris-la-opinion-senate-20151026-story.html

seamlessly incorporate during periods of lower activity. Furnishing them with compelling content and establishing designated time slots for its dissemination can be particularly effective. Strategically positioning your message is key— whether it's right before the daily news broadcast or preceding soccer games. Capitalizing on peak audience engagement moments allows your concise and impactful messages to take center stage. Ultimately, the aim is to present your message succinctly, leveraging the optimal opportunities to resonate with the audience and create a lasting impression. I'm a fan of this tactic. I've been utilizing it non-stop since Jan. 2016. It works every time you do your homework.

4. **Collaborate with community leaders:** Collaborating with respected community leaders or influencers can help you establish credibility with ethnic media outlets. Community leaders often have a strong influence on the opinions and perspectives of the community, and their endorsement or support can lend credibility to your messaging. Seek out opportunities to collaborate with community leaders and participate in community events and leverage

their influence to enhance your credibility with the ethnic media outlet.

Quick example: I like to partner with community clinics, or the local health official who is always getting media requests.

5. **Share success stories and testimonials:** Sharing success stories, testimonials, or case studies that highlight the positive impact of your work on the community can enhance your credibility. Provide concrete examples of how your efforts have benefited the community, and use testimonials from community members or organizations to reinforce your credibility. This can demonstrate the real-world impact of your work and establish you as a trusted source of information and insights. Think about offering a thank you gift card, or some type of stipend for the "real person," especially if the individual would miss time from work or family.

6. **Be responsive and engage with the community:** Responding promptly to inquiries, comments, or feedback from the ethnic media outlet and its audience is crucial

in building credibility. Engage in meaningful conversations with the community, address their concerns, and provide accurate and helpful information. This shows your commitment to the community and establishes you as an accessible and trusted source of information. Producers and reporters call me even when they know I'm not directly associated with the story they'd like to do. They call me for contacts or for ideas on how to cover a topic they know I care about.

7. **Be consistent and authentic:** Consistency and authenticity are key to establishing and maintaining credibility with ethnic media outlets.
    a. Be consistent in your messaging, values, and actions, and avoid contradictions or mixed messages.
    b. Be authentic in your approach, genuinely caring about the community, and respecting their culture, language, and values. Authenticity builds trust and enhances your credibility with the ethnic media outlet and its audience.

Remember that building credibility takes time and effort, and it requires an understanding and respect for the cultural and linguistic context of the community you are targeting.

Trusted messengers
Trusted messengers are an important part of any public information campaign, but it's especially important when developing and executing an ethnic media campaign. These people are respected in their communities and are seen as reliable sources of information.

They can be influential figures, such as activists, health professionals, religious leaders, or celebrities who are relatable to their respective communities. Their credibility can be used to spread important messages about public issues, health, safety, or other topics.

Trusted messengers are particularly important for public information campaigns because they can help to reach a wider audience. They can act as a bridge between the campaign and the people it is trying to reach. This can be especially helpful when there are languages or cultural barriers that make it difficult for a campaign to reach a certain population.

Trusted messengers can also help to increase the credibility of a message. By having a respected figure deliver a message, it can be seen as more reliable and trustworthy. This is especially important in times of crisis when people are looking for accurate and reliable information, and when misinformation is so prevalent.

It is important to stress that trusted messengers can be used to engage people on a more personal level. They can provide a human face for a campaign, which can help to make it more engaging. People are more likely to listen to someone they trust and respect.

Overall, once you identify them, they are an important tool for any public information campaign. They can help to reach a targeted audience, increase the credibility of a message, and create an engaging and personal connection with the people it is trying to reach.

CHAPTER 7

Media Relations: Building Relations

"How do you get ethnic media to cover your press events?" a colleague asked. In short, I said, most of them know my face and know who I am.

I continued explaining that, monthly, I do rounds of meet-and-greet in-person or virtual meetings. You'll be surprised how many journalists will meet with you about a topic or a service that their community needs or would be nice to have.

And of course, sometimes they will ask for advertising support, specially the very small, local publications. Most of them are for profit and most of them rely on advertising. Many times, the walls between the newsrooms and advertising are not as thick with ethnic media than as with general market media.

Building a relationship with ethnic media outlets requires effort, time, patience, and a willingness to understand the cultural nuances and values of the community they serve. Block half of a day, once a month, and get out there. Talk to them. Make yourself available for anything they need. I can tell you that would go a long way when asking journalists to attend a press event.

Here are some steps that can help you in building a strong relationship with ethnic media outlets:

1. **Research:** Identify the ethnic media outlets that are relevant to your target audience. Look for newspapers, radio stations, TV channels, or websites that cater to the specific ethnicity or language group you are interested in. Learn about their audience, editorial policies, and content preferences.
2. **If you have a paid campaign, include them.** Including a few advertising dollars as part of a public relations (PR) campaign can

offer many benefits and amplify the overall impact of the campaign. Advertising can do more than just reinforce key messages that are already being communicated through PR efforts. It can also help you get earned media coverage by letting the outlets know they are important to you, and that you are serious about investing in that community.

3. **Attend events:** Attend events hosted by ethnic media outlets to meet the staff and journalists in person. This will give you a chance to introduce yourself and your organization, and to learn more about their work and priorities.

4. **Engage with their content:** Follow them on social media even if you don't understand the language (there's usually a Google translate option). Read or watch their content regularly and engage with it on social media. Share their stories, comment on their posts, and tag them in your own content.

5. **Offer relevant content:** Provide them with relevant and timely content that would be of interest to their audience. This could be in the form of press releases, op-eds, or interviews. Make sure that the content you offer is culturally sensitive and resonates with their community.

6. **Build trust:** Be transparent and build trust by being responsive and timely in your

communication with them. Address any concerns or questions they might have and be willing to collaborate on stories and projects.
7. **Support their work:** Show your support by attending their events, sponsoring their programs, or placing ads in their publications. This will not only help you build a strong relationship, but also show your commitment to the community they serve.

Remember that building a relationship with ethnic media outlets is a long-term process that requires consistent effort and commitment. By following these steps, you can establish a strong and mutually beneficial relationship.

CHAPTER 8

Challenges When Working with Ethnic Media

IMPORTANT: ***Acknowledge inherent racial bias.***
Dear communications professional:
Before we move forward with the challenges at hand, it is time we address the elephant in the room: Everyone and anyone, at any point, can be or act racist.

Take a moment to let it sink in.

It can present itself in the shape of insensitivity, triviality, overlook, and disregard. It might even take the form of contempt when assigning a small budget of a big campaign to a conglomerate of "lesser" media outlets.

The lack of consideration for ethnic media could be due to referring to major English-only (general market) media outlets, as multicultural or omni-cultural.

The use of these false labels perpetuates the prevalent misperceptions in media representation.

It significantly undermines the crucial role of ethnic media outlets. Unless executing a highly focused media campaign, the utilization of ethnic media is redundant in the presence of "multicultural media" or whatever other term its being used to describe mainstream media.

In short, the labels of *multicultural* and *omni-cultural* are frequently used to justify the lack of diversity in advertising campaigns. As you plan a campaign, note any instances where you might use the word "them." It may be a sign of an underlying racial or ethnic bias.

Maintaining a level of awareness and discussing your ambitions can help you accomplish your objectives. If you are not a member of the community you are attempting to connect with, or even if you are, kindly take a moment to acknowledge that you may be subject to some type of inherited racism.

As an example, in Latin America, people of Indigenous descent may display racism towards others of their same race, while those with a lighter skin tone who are Black may harbor a prejudice towards those with a darker complexion.

Those in power who do not address inherent bias will significantly influence the placement of ethnic media by advertisers, leading to unequal opportunities and systemic disadvantages for marginalized communities.

The effects of racism on ethnic media placement stem from deep-seated biases, stereotypes, and discriminatory practices that pervade the advertising industry. These factors contribute to a lack of diversity, representation, and inclusivity in media campaigns, perpetuating a cycle of exclusion and underrepresentation for ethnic communities. Advertisers often allocate larger portions of their budgets to mainstream media outlets that predominantly cater to a white audience. Let's highlight that this bias stems from the misguided belief that targeting ethnic media platforms may yield lower returns on investment.

Consequently, ethnic media outlets, which serve as vital sources of information and representation for marginalized communities, face financial constraints and struggle to compete with larger mainstream channels. This lack of financial support hinders their ability to thrive and provide diverse perspectives to their respective communities.

Furthermore, racial biases in audience profiling and targeting exacerbate the disparities in ethnic media placement. Advertisers may rely on outdated or inaccurate demographic data that fails to capture the nuances and diversity within ethnic communities. As a result, they may overlook the potential of ethnic media outlets to reach and effectively engage with their intended audiences. This oversight perpetuates the notion that ethnic media is of lesser value and relevance, reinforcing the marginalization of these communities.

Stereotypes and prejudices also play a significant role in shaping advertisers' decisions regarding media placement. Preconceived notions and biases about ethnic communities can lead to the misrepresentation or underrepresentation of these groups in mainstream media.

By perpetuating stereotypes, advertisers miss the opportunity to engage with diverse and vibrant audiences, further perpetuating the cycle of exclusion. Moreover, the lack of diversity within the advertising industry itself contributes to the systemic issues affecting ethnic media placement. The underrepresentation of individuals from ethnic backgrounds in advertising agencies means that perspectives, insights, and experiences of marginalized communities may be overlooked or undervalued.

This lack of diversity in decision-making positions can perpetuate biases and hinder the adoption of more inclusive and equitable advertising practices.

To address these challenges, it is crucial for advertisers to recognize the impact of racism on ethnic media placement and take proactive steps to combat it. Advertisers should invest in diverse talent within their organizations, ensuring that decision-making positions reflect the communities they aim to reach. Additionally, developing robust audience research and targeting strategies that accurately capture the diversity within ethnic communities can help dispel stereotypes and biases.

Allocating a fair share of advertising budgets to ethnic media platforms and supporting initiatives that promote inclusivity and representation are also essential steps towards rectifying the imbalances in media placement.

Ultimately, by confronting racism in all its forms, the advertising industry can foster a more equitable and inclusive media landscape. Recognizing and challenging biases, amplifying diverse voices, and investing in ethnic media outlets can contribute to dismantling systemic barriers and promoting a more just and representative society.

SOME CHALLENGES TO OVERCOME

When working with ethnic media in a public relations campaign, there are several challenges that may arise because of various factors, some of which include:

Language and Cultural Barriers: Except for African American media outlets and some Filipino outlets, ethnic media operate in languages other than English, which can present challenges in terms of communication and understanding. Language barriers can hinder effective communication and may require additional resources, such as translation services or a trusted staff member. Additionally, cultural differences and nuances may impact the messaging and tone of the campaign, requiring careful consideration and customization.

Limited Reach and Fragmentation: Ethnic media outlets may have smaller audiences compared to mainstream media, and they may also be fragmented across different platforms, such as print, broadcast, online, and social media. This can make it challenging to reach the intended target audience and require a tailored approach to each outlet, which may increase the time and effort needed to execute a campaign effectively.

And sometimes, like in Hispanic media, there might even be media targeting specific nationalities like Salvadorans, Colombians, Guatemalans, Venezuelans, etc. This can be an asset when you are doing a very culturally targeted campaign.

Lack of Familiarity and Relationship-building: Building relationships with ethnic media outlets may require extra effort, as they may not be as well-known or familiar to the public relations team compared to mainstream media. Building trust and rapport may take time and require a deeper understanding of the outlet's audience, values, and editorial processes.

Sensitivity to Cultural Sensibilities: Ethnic communities may have unique cultural sensitivities, and public relations campaigns need to be mindful of these to avoid potential misinterpretation or offense. Understanding cultural nuances, customs, and sensitivities is crucial to avoid missteps that may negatively impact the campaign and brand reputation.

Resource Constraints: Ethnic media outlets may have limited resources, including smaller budgets, staff, and technology infrastructure. This may affect their ability to respond quickly or provide extensive coverage of a campaign. Public relations practitioners may need to be flexible and creative in finding ways to collaborate and work within these resource constraints. Be inventive and innovative.

Diversity within Ethnic Communities: Ethnic communities are diverse, with varying perspectives, opinions, and subcultures. Developing a campaign that accurately represents the diversity within an ethnic community can be challenging and requires thorough research and understanding of the target audience. For instance, oftentimes campaigns target "Asians" neglecting that the Asian community is not a monolith. The broad diversity in unique cultures, experience and looks will immediately deliver to the target Asian audience that a campaign is not aware of who they are.

Monitoring and Evaluation: Monitoring and evaluating the success of a campaign in ethnic media may be challenging because of the fragmented nature of these outlets and the availability of data and metrics. Measuring the impact and effectiveness of a campaign may require different approaches and tools to capture relevant data from multiple sources.
In every step, please, it is essential to approach ethnic media with cultural sensitivity, respect, and inclusivity to ensure the success of the campaign and build meaningful connections with diverse audiences.

How to overcome cultural differences

Here are some specific tips on how to overcome cultural difference:

1. Research the culture: Take the time to research the culture and learn about the values, beliefs, and customs of the ethnic group you are targeting. This will help you understand the nuances of the culture and create more effective outreach. It is a good idea to read about the country or geographical area where that culture developed, its challenges and successes, and the way people relate to one another.

2. Use language that resonates: When crafting messages for ethnic media outreach, use language that resonates with the target audience. This could include using specific words or phrases that are part of the culture or that are commonly used by the group. Once you've researched, test the message within that demographic to ensure the communication is hitting the mark. You can't afford to not take this key step.

3. Leverage influencers: Identify and leverage influencers within the ethnic group to help spread your message. This could include celebrities, bloggers, or other prominent figures in the community. Use radio and television personalities for your ads and for the messages. The voices people recognize.

4. Be respectful: Respect the culture and its values. Avoid any language or imagery that could be seen as offensive or insensitive.

5. Listen and adjust: Listen to feedback from the target audience and adjust your outreach accordingly. This will help you create more effective and successful outreach.

When you are targeting an ethnic community that primarily communicates in a language other than English, consider using bilingual or multilingual communications professionals that reflect the target community. It is acceptable to use someone who might not speak the native language but understands the culture and can act as your cultural broker to communicate your message. This can help bridge the language gap and establish a direct connection with the audience.

If you can, it is also a good idea to use professional translation services to ensure accuracy and authenticity in your communications, and don't stop there. Always double check translations with the target audience, a second reviewer in the community, to ensure the translations are not literal but deliver the intended sentiment. Don't rely on Google for translations. As we like to say, it's not about translation, it's about transcreation. We're not going for a literal word for word swap. We need to make sure the communication will resonate with the community.

You can also collaborate closely with ethnic media outlets to understand their editorial processes, preferences, and deadlines. Provide them with relevant and interesting content that aligns with their audience's interests.

Also, be responsive and timely. Ethnic media outlets may have tight deadlines and limited resources, so it's important to be responsive and timely in your communications. Respond promptly to inquiries, provide information and materials in a timely manner, and accommodate the outlet's editorial calendar. Being responsive and respectful of the outlet's timeline can enhance your relationship and increase the chances of coverage.

It is also important to collaborate and educate. Collaborate closely with ethnic media outlets and offer to educate them about your brand, campaign, or issue. Provide background information, context, and insights to help them better understand your messaging and objectives. Be open to answering questions, providing interviews, or participating in events or activities that can help the outlet cover your campaign more effectively.

Ensure that your campaign messaging, visuals, and strategies are inclusive and respectful of different perspectives and identities within the community.

Avoid making assumptions or generalizations, and strive to represent the diversity of the community accurately.

Finally, be sensitive to timing and events. Be aware of important cultural and religious events, holidays, and sensitive historical or social issues that may affect your outreach efforts. Avoid scheduling campaigns or events that may clash with or be insensitive to significant cultural occasions. Be mindful of the timing and context of your outreach efforts to show cultural sensitivity.

By taking these steps, you can overcome cultural differences and establish effective ethnic media outreach.

You can also offer language support. Consider providing translations of your content, press materials, and other communications to ensure that your messaging is clear and accurate. Use professional translation services to maintain quality and authenticity in your communications.

CHAPTER 9

COVID-19 Vaccines in California: A Case Study

It was December 2020. COVID-19 vaccines were approved and started being administered to medical staff and first responders. Certain ethnic groups were affected by the pandemic more than others, leading California to create Vaccinate All 58, a multilingual and multicultural COVID-19 vaccination campaign named after the state's 58 counties.

The Centers for Disease Control and Prevention (CDC) revealed data that showed that Hispanic, Pacific Islanders & Native Hawaiians, and Black people in the United States have been hospitalized at rates that are around 4-5 times higher than non-Hispanic White people.

The difference in outcomes was due to a mix of issues, like higher rates of underlying health problems, limited access to healthcare, and a greater chance of having a job that requires you to be around other people, making people more susceptible to the virus.

The VA 58 campaign effort to vaccinate various ethnic groups was the strategy to bridge this gap and make sure that those communities most affected by the pandemic could have access to the vaccine by: creating cultural and in-language content; using in-language trusted messengers; distributing information using a network of community organizations; and bringing the vaccines to the communities with pop-up clinics.

Another reason for the focus on ethnic groups was to address concerns about vaccine hesitancy. For example, despite having a high rate of vaccinations in Mexico, some Mexicans living in the United States chose not to get the vaccine. When asked why, some of them gave answers that were common among white individuals who decline to vaccinate themselves. In the Black community, the reason has to do with mistrust on the medical establishment and the way they have been mistreated in the past (Tuskegee experiment). Also, there was a lot of mistrust in other ethnic communities like the Slavic where generations of distrust with the government in Russia has led to the same mistrust in the U.S. This mistrust has led to lower rates of vaccination, which could perpetuate the disparities in COVID-19 outcomes.

To address these and other concerns, California launched a targeted outreach campaign to ensure that communities of color have access to accurate information about the safety and efficacy of the vaccine.

VA58

As mentioned, the state of California created the task force, Vaccinate All 58 Campaign, and constructed it

The Power of Ethnic Media

based on the Census 2020 best practices, which included establishing a network of Community-Based Organizations (CBO) with hundreds of ethnically diverse non-profits to directly communicate the message within their communities.

Initially, the communications unit of this Task Force was staffed, mainly, by individuals borrowed from other state agencies.

I was part of that first wave of "staff loans." I was "loaned" in February 2022 to be part of the "Earned Media and Rapid Response."

The Task Force needed people who would take the immediate challenge of funneling information to all the different outlets in the state and respond in real time to the thirst that reporters had about what California was doing to vaccinate all, regardless of their ability to make an appointment or to actually get to a vaccination site.

The Power of Ethnic Media

Let's remember that when the COVID-19 vaccine became available in December 2020, the front-line workers and essential workers were priority. As supply became available, in March 2021, mega vaccinations sites opened, some by FEMA and some by the counties. But to make an appointment, people needed access to a computer or smartphone, and most times a car or a ride.

After those chaotic moments, and once California started getting larger amounts of vaccines, we could scale it down from massive sites to pop-up vaccination clinics.

All those different phases required a strong communications campaign. And we had it. A group of strong women within the government led the communications campaign. The primary messages were that we will all get vaccinated, we all just need to be patient, and we need wait our turn. That's why the website is still called "MyTurn.ca.gov."

The Power of Ethnic Media

As I have expertise in Spanish news, I was brought on board to act as a spokesperson and lead the rapid Spanish earned media response.

I started asking questions about other earned ethnic media efforts. In December 2021, I was appointed as the Multiethnic Press Secretary to the Vaccinate All 58 campaign, which in the summer of 2022, changed to the Office of Community Partnership and Strategic Communications.

There has been less of an argument against ethnic media in government communication in the past couple of years, and this can be attributed to the success of vaccinating underserved communities.

Some people might argue that there are still many people who have not gotten vaccinated against COVID-19, but to that, I must insist that:

- Everyone who wanted the vaccines, has gotten the vaccine.
- Anyone who didn't have a car and wanted a vaccine, has received it.

- Anyone who does not speak English and wanted a vaccine, has gotten information they needed to decide.

Examining a Statewide Communication Plan Aimed at Connecting with Varied Audiences During the Coronavirus Outbreak

In response to the COVID-19 pandemic, California launched a comprehensive earned media campaign to reach its diverse population and encourage vaccination. The campaign aimed to address vaccine hesitancy and misinformation, as well as to promote vaccination to protect public health.

The campaign employed a variety of tactics to engage audiences across different ethnic groups, languages, and regions, focusing on building trust and relationships with local community leaders and organizations.

California has a diverse population, with a significant proportion of residents who are Hispanic/Latino, Asian American and Pacific Islander (AAPI),

Black/African American, and Native American[16]. Together they are over half of the state's population. The pandemic brought to light the existing discrepancy regarding access to healthcare and healthcare services.

We gave priority to these segments of the population to make sure everyone had equitable access to vaccination and to reduce any disparities.

We identified vaccine hesitancy and misinformation, amplified by the pandemic and the proliferation of online platforms, as a need to address.

To address these challenges, and in collaboration with several PR ethnic-focused agencies under the umbrella of the advertising agency Runyon Saltzman, Inc. (RSE), an earned media campaign was created and adjusted constantly to reflect the day by day

---

[16] United States Census Bureau. 2020 statistics.
https://data.census.gov/profile/California?g=040XX00US06

changes we were all seeing and experimenting. The aim was to build trust and credibility with diverse audiences through a range of tactics and channels.

We were responding almost in real time and pivoting at every turn.

The days were long, the weekends almost non-existing… for a few months. Media wanted to know what the State was doing and why, constantly.

Tactics

The campaign employed a range of tactics to reach diverse audiences, including cultivating and maintaining a list of credible community spokespeople, prioritizing earned media outreach efforts, securing interviews for state doctors and trusted spokespeople like Dr. Ilan Shapiro, from a network of clinics in Los Angeles County called AltaMed.

Also, we provided earned media support for community-based events and vaccine clinics, holding community conversations with over 400 ethnic media partners across all markets and in many languages.

We also created an ethnic media journalist support program. We named it Myth Busters Fellowships. Under this program, we provided financial support to 58 reporting projects to address vaccines misinformation. We did not tell them what to write. We did not edit their stories. We provided reporting parameters, topic, experts, and deadlines[17].
We also collaborated with community-based organizations on art installations.

Every month, from February 2021 to the end of the summer of that year, we held press briefing statewide and regional, and in different languages, to facilitate partnerships with media outlets and other organizations. And yes, there were a lot of press releases that were translated and other pre-written

---

[17] "Covid Myth Busters." Ethnic Media Services. 2022-2023. https://ethnicmediaservices.org/covid-myth-busters-4/

content as well as pre-recorded video testimonials with spokespeople that reflected the community.

As mentioned before, one of the key tactics was the cultivation and maintenance of a list of community spokespeople, which comprised over 160 people from diverse backgrounds and communities.

These spokespeople were identified and vetted based on their credibility and influence in their respective communities, and were engaged actively to provide feedback, advice, and support for the campaign. The spokespeople were also leveraged for media interviews, social media content, and community outreach activities.

Another key tactic was the prioritization of earned media outreach efforts, which were organized into 20 "weeks of action" that included one per month, as well as a series of weeks of action related to the "Kids and Family Sprint." Each week of action had a specific theme or message that was tailored to the target audience and was supported by a range of earned media activities, such as press releases, media pitches, op-eds, social media content, and community events.

Just a quick note here that op-eds do not work for all ethnic media segments. AAPI and African Americans weeklies are more open to them than Spanish-language media. It is worth noting that not all Spanish publications contain opinion pages. Those that do, such as *La Opinión*, require a great deal of patience and the ability to convey ideas within a limited word count in order to be published.

Results

The state's vaccination campaign vaccinated about 72% of the population, at least with the first doses. It is hard to say the overall impact of the state's paid and earned efforts, plus all the localized efforts, but what I can say is that state and local did their part to make sure that everyone had access.

From a PR front, we prioritized:

- Community-based events and vaccine clinics, prioritizing zip codes with low vaccination rates.
- Community conversations across all markets and in many different languages.
- Gave out Myth Buster fellowships to ethnic media reporters.
- Secured interviews with state doctors, local doctors, and other trusted spokespeople.
- Supported artistic efforts in communities that promote vaccination.
- Secured partnerships in-language with over ethnic media outlets, creating long format discussions to bring along people who still had questions about the mRNA vaccines.

Examples of specific tactics

Las Posadas con Vacunas

During December 2021 and 2022, we partnered with a Central American-oriented television show to organize community events in an area of Los Angeles with a below-average rate of vaccination. We called it "*Las Posadas con Vacunas,*" which was a mix of a traditionally and culturally adapted reenactment of

Virgin's Mary and Joseph traveling to Bethlehem during the Roman Census, plus a vaccination clinic. On every occasion, the broadcast was live streamed by the TV program via their Facebook page and a local TV station televised during the Christmas period it. At each of the events, on average, 50+ people were vaccinated who would have otherwise gone without, in addition to those that were influenced after seeing it on television and/or social media.

Ding Ding TV Special

During Dec 2021, we partnered with a Chinese television program in the Bay Area, Ding Ding TV, to discuss the value of vaccination, especially for individuals with underlying medical issues, because we knew that television and YouTube was an effective way to communicate with the Chinese population in the area and raise understanding about the advantages of immunization.

Working with a university professor who is knowledgeable about vaccination and its benefits and can speak Cantonese was extremely helpful in

providing accurate and up-to-date information to the viewers. The professor is a trusted in-language spokesperson and could address concerns that the community had about the vaccine.
Partnering with a TV show was a smart move, as it allows you to reach a larger audience and spread your message effectively.

With the help of the show, we promoted the importance of vaccination and encouraged people to get vaccinated. Overall, this initiative was a great way to promote public health and safety, and it can have a significant impact on the community's willingness to get vaccinated and protect themselves against COVID-19.

Fellowships (Myth Buster)[18]
Changes in the industry are having a large effect on ethnic media, like other news media, with reduced

---

[18] "Covid Myth Busters." Ethnic Media Services. 2022-2023. https://ethnicmediaservices.org/covid-myth-busters-4/

staff and capabilities. Through Ethnic Media Services, we provided 48 fellowships to journalists, which act as a financial motivation to write about a particular topic. We do not have control over what gets published, but you can support and guide the story by making experts and data available.

The topic was to debunk myths in their specific communities. The journalist and outlet chose the myths that were affecting the vaccination rate within their ethnic group and wrote about it in a way that the story did not amplify the myth. EMS had a workshop to cover misinformation about the horrible and unwanted side effects of accidentally amplifying myths or disinformation which served as the first framework of the program.

Spanish Media COVID-19 Vaccine Telethons
With the increasing availability of COVID-19 vaccines and news directors' support, I created and implemented a TV program called "*Línea de Ayuda.*" This program, like telethons, focused on scheduling vaccine appointments. A telethon is usually a televised

event that typically lasts for several hours or even days to raise awareness or money, for a particular cause or charity.

In our case, the telethon format was used to answer questions with the aim of scheduling COVID-19 vaccination appointments. A typical telethon usually involves a host or group of hosts who appeal to viewers. During the VA58 telethons, the host was the news anchors or reporters and usually took place during the event. During the first *Línea de Ayuda* the call to action started at 12:00 pm, and extended until 7 or 8 pm.

In our different telethons across the state, the anchors or reporters often shared interesting vaccination stories and interview medical doctors or VA58 spokesperson.

Among the participating television stations were:
1. Telemundo Los Angeles
2. Telemundo San Diego
3. Telemundo Bay Area
4. Telemundo Sacramento
5. Telemundo Fresno
6. Entravision- Univision San Diego
7. Entravision- Univision Palm Springs

8. Entravision- Univision Santa Barbara
9. NBC Los Angeles
10. NBC San Diego
11. NBC Bay Area

Sample of one day event:

Some telethons started at 12:00 pm during the midday newscast; others at 4:00 pm with the afternoon newscast. Most ended at 7 pm or 8 pm, when the afternoon newscast wrapped up.

- 12:00 pm- midday newscast - interview during segment 1 or 2 with subject matter expert or spokesperson.
- 12:30 pm- 30-sec promo announcing the *Línea de ayuda* airs 2x or 3x.
- 1:00 pm - 4:00 pm – 30-sec promo announcing the *Línea de ayuda* airs 2x or 3x.
- 4:00 pm- anchor opens up the newscast announcing the *Línea de ayuda* and asking people to call with questions.
- 4:30 pm- anchor or reporter interviews a subject matter expert or spokesperson.
- 5:00 pm - another interview or a testimonial often during first or second segment.
- 5:30 pm - anchor continues announcing the phone line and encourages people to call in with their questions or to make appointments.
- 6:00 pm - this is the highest rating news hour. Anchor announces the phone line and asks people to call in with questions. During first and/or second segment interviews, a subject matter expert or spokesperson.
- 6:00-7:00 pm- 30-sec promo announcing the *Línea de ayuda* airs 2x or 3x.

VA58 provided:

Our own help line with operators that answered the phone in Spanish during the phone events: 833-606-2880. The networks posted on social media, CDPH and our network of community based organizations did the same too. The art was provided by the newsrooms.

When NBC stations joined, we used the regular MyTurn phone line were the operators answer in English.

Unquestionable results

We received thousands of calls from Spanish speakers in 2021, and we scheduled hundreds of appointments, including multiple appointments from the same household.

In 2022, the number of calls dropped significantly because of a decrease of interest and the fact that most people who wanted to get vaccinated already had their shots.

Thank you!
I believe this quick how-to guide can be the beginning of your new ethnic media strategy. If have questions, it does not hurt to ask from a position of learning. Don't assume. It's allowed and encouraged to ask someone with a different experience, gender, culture, ethnicity, and values about their experience so that we can create a more inclusive communication for all.

ABOUT THE AUTHOR

Yurina Melara Valiulis, MS, Ph.D. is an experienced media communications strategist with over two decades of experience in journalism and media relations. She currently serves as the Multiethnic Press Secretary for a California state agency.

An award-winning journalist, Melara has worked on multiple TV shows in Los Angeles as both a talent and producer and was a public health reporter for *La Opinion* from 2005 to 2015.

She is a passionate advocate for equity and representation in media and volunteers as the Diversity, Equity, and Inclusion Committee Chair and as part of the Board of Directors of the Public Relations Society of America Los Angeles.

Melara lives in Los Angeles with her husband, two children, and three cats.

The Power of Ethnic Media

FOLLOW ME ON AMAZON

CHECK OUT MY NEW AUTHOR PAGE ON AMAZON.COM!

HTTPS://WWW.AMAZON.COM/AUTHOR/YURINAMELARA

www.yurinamelara.com

OTHER BOOKS BY THE AUTHOR

Whose Life Is It Anyway?
Yurina Melara

Whose Life Is It Anyway? | Kindle Vella

IN 1996 EL SALVADOR, A JOURNALIST NAMED MARIANA IS CAUGHT UP IN THE NATION'S STRUGGLE. IN A COUNTRY WHERE TRADITION AND MODERNITY CLASH, THE REPORTER NAVIGATES A WORLD ON THE BRINK OF TRANSFORMATION. ABORTION, ONCE LEGALLY ACCESSIBLE FOR MEDICAL REASONS, IS FACING AN UNCERTAIN FATE AS A NEW LAW THREATENS TO EXTINGUISH THE FLAME OF CHOICE ALTOGETHER. ABORTION RIGHTS ARE BEING THREATENED BY A GROUP OF RICH STAY-AT-HOME WIVES WITH A RELIGIOUS AGENDA.

TODO PERSONAL ES UNA NOVELA NEGRA QUE TOMA LUGAR EN EL SALVADOR. LOS ASESINATOS DE UNA MAMÁ Y UNA NIÑA DE SIETE AÑOS FRENTE A UN COLEGIO EN SAN SALVADOR, LLEVARÁ AL ESPOSO Y PADRE, DARWIN —UN EX PANDILLERO CONVERTIDO EN REDENTOR— A FORMAR UNA ALIANZA POCO COMÚN CON UN INVESTIGADOR DE LA POLICÍA Y UNA PERIODISTA. ¿QUIÉN ESTÁ DETRÁS DE LOS ASESINATOS? ¿Y POR QUÉ? ESTA NOVELA DE SUSPENSO TE ATRAPARÁ ENTRE LO QUE DEBERÍA SER, LA JUSTICIA SALVADOREÑA Y LA JUSTICIA DIVINA.

Made in the USA
Columbia, SC
17 January 2024

f8dff5ab-126b-4b98-b694-17697c464b98R01